© 1992 Franklin Watts

Franklin Watts
96 Leonard Street
London EC2A 4RH

Franklin Watts Australia
14 Mars Road
Lane Cove
NSW 2066

UK ISBN: 0 7496 0776 9

A CIP catalogue record for this book is available
from the British Library.

Editor: Sarah Ridley
Designer: Janet Watson
Illustrator: Linda Costello

Photographs: Eye Ubiquitous 18, 20; Geo-Science
Features Picture Library 13, 15 (top right), Geo-
Science Features Picture Library/Dr B Booth 15
(bottom left), 15 (bottom right); Robert Harding
Picture Library cover, 7, 10, 25, 28; Hutchison
Library title page, 16; ZEFA 8, 15 (top left), 23, 26.

Printed in Malaysia

LIFT OFF!

UNDER THE GROUND

Joy Richardson

FRANKLIN WATTS
London ● New York ● Sydney ● Toronto

Beneath our feet

We live with our heads
in the air and our
feet on the ground.

We dig into the ground
to make the foundations
for our houses and roads.

Many people have lived
on the earth before us.
Ruined houses, old coins
and broken pots now lie
buried in the ground.

In the soil beneath our feet we
may find the remains of the past.

Soil

The planet earth has a thin coating of
soil in which plants can grow.
Without soil, the earth
would be a rocky desert.

Soil forms slowly.
It is mostly made of broken rock.
Dead plants and animals rot away and
mix with the rock to form soil.

Worms wriggle through
the soil and break it up.
Rabbits and foxes burrow into
the soil to make their homes.

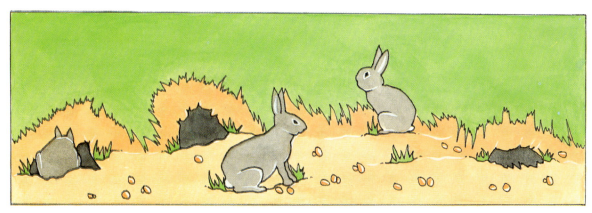

The earth's crust

Beneath the soil lies the
earth's rocky crust.

This was formed millions of years ago,
when fiery hot liquid
slowly cooled into hard rock.

Huge plates of rock covered
the earth's surface like
jigsaw puzzle pieces.

When the rocky plates slid
against each other,
mountains were pushed up.

Volcanoes

When the earth was new,
it was covered with volcanoes.

Volcanoes are mountains
which push up through
cracks in the earth's crust.

Hot gas and ash
explode through the crack.
Liquid rock called lava
pours out and makes new rock.

Some volcanoes still explode
from time to time.

Minerals and crystals

Rocks are like cakes.
They are made of a mix of
ingredients called minerals.
The mineral mix is cooked
inside the earth.

You can see a mix of
mineral crystals in granite.

Some rocks contain crystals of
precious stones such as diamonds.

Metal minerals, such as
iron or silver, may be
mixed in with the rock.

rock crystals

granite

uncut and cut
diamonds

silver ore
in rock

New rocks for old

Rocks are worn away
by wind and water and
broken into tiny grains.

Grains of sand and clay
settle in layers at
the bottom of the sea.
The dead remains of sea creatures
sink into the layers.

The layers press down
and stick together.
Over many years, they turn into stone.
The creatures become stony fossils.

It takes a very long time
for new rock to form.

Rocks on the move

We can now walk over rock
which used to be covered by the sea.
This is why fossils may
be found on rocky hilltops.

Pressure under the earth
pushes huge plates of rock
up, down or sideways,
or folds them into hills.

Earthquakes can crack
the earth's crust and
make parts rise or fall.

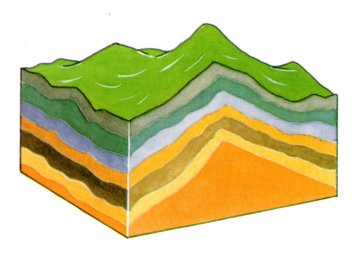

Stone quarry

The rock beneath us can be used
to make roads and buildings.

Stone is cut out of
the ground in quarries.

Soft chalky rock can be
used to make cement.
Layers of pebbles and bits of rock
make gravel for the roads.

Solid blocks of stone are
cut to make buildings.

Coal

In some places there are
layers of coal between
the layers of rock.

Millions of years ago,
trees and plants decayed
and were covered in water.
Sand and mud pressed down on top.

Slowly the sand and mud
hardened into stone.
The remains of the plants
hardened into coal.

Coalminers cut out the coal
from between the layers of rock
and bring it up to the surface.

Oil

Oil is another fuel which
may be found between layers of rock.

Millions of years ago, tiny creatures
sank to the bottom of the sea and
were buried by sand and mud.
Very slowly, the dead creatures
turned into drops of oil.

Oil wells are sunk into the rock
in land or under the sea.
The oil is collected
through long pipelines.

Oil rigs float on the water
above the oil well.

Underground water

Rain soaks into the ground
and trickles down through
loose stones and soft rock.

Water can wear rock away
and make caves and tunnels.

When water drips down through
limestone it collects minerals
which form long stalagmites
and stalactites in caves.

When water reaches
a layer of rock which
it cannot pass through,
it makes an underground lake.

Underground paths

Engineers cut underground tunnels.
Miners collect coal and metal.
Explorers investigate caves.
People drill deep for oil.

But no-one has ever got deeper
than the top layers of the
earth's thin outer crust.

Scientists can only make guesses
about the hot heavy rock beneath,
and the earth's metal core.

Index